Contents

WITHDRAWN

Acknowledgements
Original text by Kevin Hickey MBE
(former Amateur Boxing Association of
England Ltd (ABAE) National Coach,
and Technical Director of the British
Olympic Association). Additional
material by Alan Sanigar (ABAE Coach
Educator); article on Women's Boxing
by Raine New. Approved by Amateur
Boxing Association of England Ltd.

Cover photography by Empics.
Photograph on inside back cover and
pages 7, 8, 24 and 33 courtesy of Getty
Images. All other photographs courtesy
of Tim Strange. Thank you to all the
boxers, coaches and clubs involved for
their time and expertise.
Illustrations by Dave Saunders.

*Photograph on inside front cover: Fitzroy
Lodge A.B.C. (London). One of the oldest
boxing gyms in the country.*

1

Foreword

Know The Game Boxing provides an excellent introduction and development pathway for a wide range of ages and abilities, helping participants to understand and practise the fundamental skills of boxing. From getting started at the local Amateur Boxing Association (ABA) club to progressing as a professional, the basics done well are a must, and Kevin Hickey and Alan Sanigar, the co-authors of this book, have gone to some length to explain this through detailed text and illustrated photographs.

The challenge for boxing skills commences at the ABA club, and there are some 600 spread throughout the country. Here, the beginner, through careful guidance, can benefit from the fitness factors connected with boxing training, as well as enjoying recreational programmes. Those who wish to progress to the competition arena can do so by sparring practice and a more intensive programme of preparation, as explained in this book.

Kevin Hickey (ABAE National Coach, 1969–89) wrote the first edition of *Know The Game Boxing* almost 20 years ago, and while much of the text still stands up to scrutiny, Alan Sanigar has taken on the task of updating it and has to be congratulated for his painstaking efforts.

Alan Sanigar is the ABAE Coach Educator, and certainly knows his stuff when it comes to discussing the technical issues associated with boxing. He has been an advanced coach for over 25 years, and for a period during those years was regional coach for the Western Counties ABA prior to taking up his present position. You can therefore progress with confidence in the knowledge that what you read in this book is of sound material.

Ian Irwin
ABA Performance Director

Introduction

Boxing is a highly individual sport. The all-round fitness required is second to none, which is why 'Keep fit boxing' is becoming increasingly popular. The technical and tactical skills needed for success in competition come only with extreme dedication. The strength and resolve of boxers are indicative of the unique character-building attributed to the sport.

Boxing styles

'Styles make fights'
Anon

The higher the level of competition, the more a boxer will need to vary his tactics. The following are some basic style guidelines.

Invariably, the most entertaining contests are between a stylish 'boxer' and a strong 'fighter' – the worst are often between two 'counter-punchers'.

- **'Fighter'** or **'Puncher'** – an aggressive, two-fisted, all-action style. Often used by boxers shorter in stature than their opponent, they usually press forwards, often willing to take a few punches to get in close with their more powerful hooks and uppercuts. A granite chin is essential.

- **'Boxer'** or **'Stylist'** – a defensive style. Footwork skills are used along with long-range boxing. The emphasis is on an 'educated jab'. The stylist looks to present a moving target and to win on points.

- **'Counter puncher'** – tries to cause his opponent to miss before countering, then gets out of the way. Counter punchers are often 'southpaws' too (*see* page 13). The more experienced can counter moving forward, triggering off their opponent, as well as on the back foot.

- **'Box-fighter'** – a combination of **'Fighter'** and **'Boxer'**. The box-fighter selects when to 'box' or 'fight'. For many coaches this is the ideal boxing style.

- **'Flash'** – an unorthodox boxer who 'breaks the rules', keeping hands low and switching stance (southpaw to orthodox) etc. He has natural ability in abundance – speed, agility, a good eye and timing. It's when he meets someone faster or stronger that the problems can set in!

- **'High-tempo'** (usually in the lighter weight groups) – a bustling style, relying on a high volume punch rate to unsettle opponents. Needless to say – they must be super fit!

During the ebb and flow of a closely matched contest, top performers can often call on a 'bit of everything' listed – the unpredictable style!

Amateur and professional boxing

The main visual difference between amateur and professional boxers is that amateurs wear vests, head-guards and often white tipped gloves.

Other differences:

	Amateur	Professional
Length of rounds	2 mins (senior)	2–3 mins
	1½ mins (child)	
Number of rounds	3 to 4	4 to 12
Weight of gloves	10 oz (340 g)	8 oz up to Welterweight
		10 oz over Welterweight
Head-guard	yes	none
Vest	yes	none
Weight groups	11 (*see* page 5)	16 (*see* page 5)
World titles	1	4 (major titles)

The rules

The rules of amateur and professional boxing are much the same, but their emphasis and interpretation can vary a lot. In general, referees of amateur boxing apply rules more rigidly, particularly relating to holding. In professional fights this is virtually ignored, and is often regarded as a legitimate tactic (sometimes called 'claiming'), but excessive use can be penalised and a point deducted as a result.

The weights

In 2003, amateur boxing had to reduce its weights by one category for the Olympic Games. This resulted in the removal of light middleweight: 71 kg.

The amateur and professional weights listed are all upper limits. If in a championship contest a boxer weighed in on the official scales even fractionally over the limit, he would not be eligible to participate in the contest.

Amateur	Upper limit	Professional	Upper limit
Light flyweight	up to 48 kg	Strawweight	
Flyweight	51 kg	(World, not Britain)	105 lb
Bantamweight	54 kg	Junior flyweight	
Featherweight	57 kg	(World not Britain)	108 lb
Lightweight	60 kg	Flyweight	8 st
Light welterweight	64 kg	Bantamweight	8 st 6 lb
Welterweight	69 kg	Super bantamweight	8 st 10 lb
Middleweight	75 kg	Featherweight	9 st
Light heavyweight	81 kg	Super featherweight	9 st 4 lb
Heavyweight	91 kg	Lightweight	9 st 9 lb
Super heavyweight	over 91 kg	Light welterweight	10 st
		Welterweight	10 st 7 lb
		Junior middleweight	11 st
		Middleweight	11 st 6 lb
		Super middleweight	12 st
		Light heavyweight	12 st 7 lb
		Cruiserweight	13 st 8 lb
		Heavyweight	13st 8 lb plus

Women's boxing

Although women boxed at a demonstration event in the 1904 Olympic Games in St Louis, USA, it was not until 1997 that the first amateur female bout took place in Britain. At the time it was estimated that approximately 500 women were participating within the sport in England, but only a small percentage of these were training to compete.

Yet other countries were already holding boxing competitions: Sweden was first in 1988, while the first international event was held at the Acropolis Cup in Athens in 1997. And in 2001, America hosted the first Women's World Championships.

The majority of women participating within the sport today do so for personal fitness rather than in competition. However, due to public demand, the first National Championships took place in England in May 2003.

Making a start

There are two ways of actively participating in amateur boxing: recreationally and competitively. Many amateur boxing clubs (ABCs) offer both, run by Amateur Boxing Association of England (ABAE) Ltd qualified coaches.

Recreational boxing

A non-contact approach to boxing, this involves all the training aspects except sparring. For the young there are two award schemes: 'Kid Gloves' (ABAE) and 'Schools Standard Scheme' (Schools ABA). For seniors there is the 'Lonsdale Golden Gloves'.

These staged skills development awards can be used purely for recreational boxing or as a stepping stone to competition readiness. Contact ABAE or the Schools ABA for further details (*see* page 47).

Competitive boxing

You will be matched according to weight, experience, and, for youngsters in particular, age. Most clubs take novices to tournaments before their first contest to soak up the atmosphere, so that when their big day arrives they are familiar with the proceedings.

Your coach will tell you when you're ready to compete technically (skills in attack and defence), physically (stamina, strength) and psychologically. In order to participate in competitive boxing, it is necessary to have a medical card.

Medical card

Before a boxer receives a medical card to certify that he is fit to box, he has to undergo a thorough medical examination. He also has to be examined every time he boxes. Once he has passed the medical he is weighed. In championships, the exact weight group limit has to be made. Once a competitor has competed in a certain weight group, if in a subsequent round he fails to make the limit, he is ineligible to continue. In club tournaments, the weight categories are less strictly adhered to, but there are rules in place about weight differences between competitors.

The medical card has complete details of the boxer's record, including the names of his previous opponents. This enables fairness in matching. Matches are made prior to the shows, but some are changed on the night.

Whether you are interested in recreational or competitive boxing, contact your national governing body for details of your nearest boxing club (*see* page 47).

What to wear

Training

You don't need much specialist equipment – tracksuit, trainers, t-shirt and shorts are ideal. Well-fitting footwear and clean cotton socks are recommended, as early footwork practice can cause friction and blisters for the unaccustomed. Velpeau crepe bandage (2.5 m) for hand protection and support can be purchased from most chemists. The gloves, bag, mitts and skipping ropes are usually supplied by the club.

Competition

Again, most of the equipment is supplied, including gloves, head-guards and protectors. You will need the club vest and boxing shorts, and boxing boots are recommended for the ankle support they give. Finally, a gumshield is mandatory and should ideally be individually fitted.

Officials

Referee

He is in overall control of the contest, making sure both boxers adhere strictly to the rules.

Judges

There are between three and five judges in amateur boxing; three in professional boxing. Judges score the contest. In the UK there are no draws – a winner must be declared.

Official in charge (OIC)

The official in charge of the whole tournament – the buck stops with him.

Clerk of scales

Responsible for weighing in and matching the boxers (with the OIC) at the set time.

Master of ceremonies (MC)

Announces the boxers at the start of the contest and the decision at the end.

Recorder

Keeps a complete record of all the tournament bouts and results, and is responsible for the medical cards.

Medical officer

A qualified medical officer has to be present throughout all tournaments and for the boxers' medical examinations. Paramedics should also be in attendance.

The contest

Contrary to media caricatures, the knockout is rare. The vast majority of decisions are made on points.

Scoring points

A definition of a scoring blow is one delivered with the knuckle part of the glove on the target area with force (while no foul is being committed).

Amateur contests

In both international and national championships computer scoring is used. The judges (usually five of them) press a red or blue button for a scoring blow. When a majority press within a second of each other, the score registers for that boxer.

A hand-held scoring machine is used for all tournaments in which a computer is not used.

The hand-held scoring machine has red and blue buttons which the judge uses to record the scoring blows. At the end of the contest the judge records the score on the score paper (*see* fig. 1) and hands this to the referee. The machine also has warning buttons for red and blue. When one of the buttons is pressed, 2 points are added to the opponent's score. In addition, if the referee gives the boxer a warning and the majority of judges agree, 2 points are awarded to the opponent.

Professional contests

These are scored manually: 10 points are awarded to the winner of a round, 9 or less to the loser. A knockdown scores a full point and often wins the round – unless, of course, your opponent returns the compliment . . .

AMATEUR BOXING ASSOCIATION OF ENGLAND

Bout Number ....

Boxer's Names
....

▮▮▮▮▮ Colour ▮▮▮▮▮

Nation
....

WxJ	Points	Points	WxJ
Total			Total

Remarks when points are equal	L.S.D.

Decision

Winner ....

Judge"s Signature ....

Judge"s Name ....
(Print)

▲ *Fig. 1   The score paper*

Boxing skills

Target area – lines of attack

The target area is shown in fig. 2. Only punches delivered with the knuckle part of the glove on the shaded area score. Both the head and body need to be protected from attack, which can be made with straight or hook (bent arm) punches. The latter are especially dangerous, as they tend to come around a defender's glove and outside the line of vision. Uppercuts are thrown vertically in between the guard. Punches landing on the arms and shoulders do not score.

Lines of attack

Hooks (around the gloves): shaded arrows.
Straight punches to head and body: straight arrows.
Uppercuts to head and body: blue arrows.
Hooks to the body and steep hooks to the head are not shown: they are thrown at 45-degree angles inside and under the guard.

▶ *Fig. 2 The target area*

Scoring a hit

The aim is to land the knuckle part of the closed glove on the target area. Punches delivered with any other part of the glove are fouls – they do not score, and in competition the referee will caution the offender.

Making a fist

First, try making a fist without wearing the glove. Tuck the thumb comfortably around the fingers so that it does not project beyond the line of knuckles. Your fist should be lightly clenched until impact.

Punching in a straight line

All straight punches should aim to travel in a straight line from the shoulder. Notice that on impact the back of the hand continues this 'power line'. The fist rotates before impact.

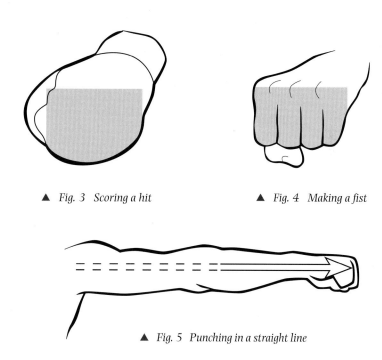

▲ *Fig. 3 Scoring a hit*　　　　▲ *Fig. 4 Making a fist*

▲ *Fig. 5 Punching in a straight line*

11

Stance and guard

A boxer who leads with his left is called an orthodox boxer. A boxer who leads with his right is called a southpaw. The illustrations show how an orthodox boxer stands. All boxers should stand in a sideways position, giving maximum protection of the target area with the arms and shoulders, while allowing attack or countering with either hand. Not that all boxers should adopt the same stance – in fact taller boxers should stand more sideways. This is because a taller boxer should develop a stance which makes best use of his height and reach. His main punch will be the jab, while the shorter boxer will be trying to adopt a two-fisted approach.

Coaching hints

- **Head:** chin protected by left shoulder; look up at opponent 'through your eyebrows'.
- **Trunk:** turned in alignment with the feet to close the target area.
- **Arms:** held loose and relaxed, with elbows positioned to protect the body.
- **Hands:** held partly open or loosely closed in optimum position for defence and punch.
- **Feet:** approximately shoulder width apart; front foot turned at 45 degrees from the opponent with back foot angled further away and back heel raised. Knees flexed with a greater degree of bend in the back leg.
- **Balance:** Necessary at all times to enable you to move quickly in any direction. Your body weight should be transferred as you take evasive action to avoid punches. Body weight is transferred laterally when slipping, and shifted backwards on to the back foot with the layback, but should not shift too far forwards as this causes the boxer to lose balance and can put the head in a vulnerable and potentially 'illegal' position.

Stance and guard (side)

Southpaws

A boxer who leads with his right hand and stands with his right foot forward is called a southpaw. Usually – though not always – boxers who are left-handed find that this style suits them best. Both orthodox and southpaw stances should be tried before deciding which feels more comfortable. The same coaching points hold for both styles.

Many southpaw boxers are counter-punchers – they make their opponent lead before throwing the counter punch. Good balance and sound foot-work is therefore especially important. A good southpaw can counter whilst moving in any direction, using either hand or both, in a counter combination. However, southpaws come in as many varied styles as orthodox boxers.

Stance and guard (facing)

Stance and guard (southpaw)

13

Footwork

Forwards and backwards

All basic footwork should consist of short sliding movements, with balance maintained throughout. Your feet should never cross or cause the base to narrow or overstretch. A good test is whether you can use either hand to attack or counter against your opponent at all times. Rhythm and speed are needed to move either into attack or away from your opponent's attack. You should aim to maintain the optimum distance between your feet at all times.

Moving forwards, the front foot leads with the back foot following, covering exactly the same distance as the front foot. Momentum comes from a push with the back leg.

Moving backwards, the rear foot leads with the front foot following. The front foot provides the drive and snaps into the 'on guard' distance as quickly as possible.

▲ *Fig. 5   Moving forwards*

▲ *Fig. 6   Moving backwards*

Coaching hints

- Remember: 'the punch follows the feet'. If the feet are incorrectly placed, a faulty punch will follow. Time spent practising footwork is never wasted.
- Practising facing and sideways on to a mirror will help a boxer see for himself., while the lines of the gym floor can be used to check the distance covered by each foot.
- More advanced practices can include varying the speed of movement.

Lateral

The orthodox boxer will generally experience greater difficulty in moving to his right, the southpaw to his left. Moving to the left and right is important to both styles. Lateral (sideways) movement will enable a boxer to launch his attack or counter-attack from a different angle, as well as making him a more difficult target to hit.

For movement both to left and right, the same principles apply. Moving to the left, the left foot leads; moving to the right, the right foot leads. Only a few inches are covered at a time, with the trailing foot snapping into position and retaining complete balance. Keep the feet close to the floor in a sliding action.

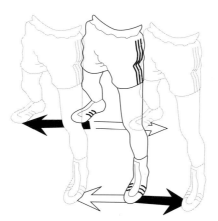

▲ *Fig. 7 Moving laterally*

Coaching hints

● The bend in your rear leg should be kept throughout, ready to push forwards or drive a punch with the rear hand.
● Once the essential 'left and right' movement has been mastered, you can try circling both ways around your opponent. A spot on the floor can substitute.

Moving continually in one direction comes easily (and is predictable and easy to read). The real skill is the ability to change direction rapidly – to turn defence to attack and attack to defence seamlessly.

Punches

The jab

The jab to the head is the most important punch in boxing. All boxers need to have a quality jab. Not only is it the chief points scorer, but it creates the openings for the rear hand. Using the hand nearest your opponent, it gives him less chance to react. Practices should be used to develop the art of feinting, with which you can keep your opponent guessing.

Once the attacker is in range, your leading hand snaps away from your side with the trunk pivoting at speed. Power comes from a quarter turn of your leading shoulder. The wrist turns just before impact to land with the palm facing the floor. After landing the glove returns along exactly the same path.

Coaching hints

● Practise punching at the open glove of a partner's rear hand from a standing position. Add the foot movement as soon as the essential 'feel' of the punch has been acquired.
● The non-punching hand guards the chin throughout, with the chin receiving extra protection from the leading shoulder.
● The jab is driven in line with the shoulder, with the arm relaxed until impact. Only when the leading foot has slid into position should the punch be thrown – at speed!
● With the opponent (target) moving forwards (coming on to the punch), judgement of distance and timing are needed.

● Once the basic jab has been learnt, different types of jabs can be mastered by varying the speed and power of the punch. Openings will occur both for fast, light scoring jabs and for solid jabs to keep your opponent off-balance.

Left jab to the head ▶

The straight right

The orthodox boxer's straight right to the head can be either a power or a scoring punch. Usually it follows a jab which has measured the distance for the right to follow. Practice on a light punch bag will help develop both speed and accuracy of punch. As you progress, technical and tactical skills are developed with coach pads, partner work and sparring.

Power comes from your right foot, which drives the right side forward in a hips-trunk-arm sequence. The explosive drive off the back foot transfers the weight to the left leg, being driven against a firm left side. As with the jab, the right glove turns before impact to land palm facing the floor.

Southpaw boxers can apply the same principles to the left hand and follow the coaching points.

Coaching hints

- Measure the distance with the leading hand.
- Drive from the right foot, pivoting at speed.
- Keep the left side firm.
- Hit through the target.
- Left hand remains 'on guard'.
- After impact the right glove turns to the defending position.

Straight right to the head ▶

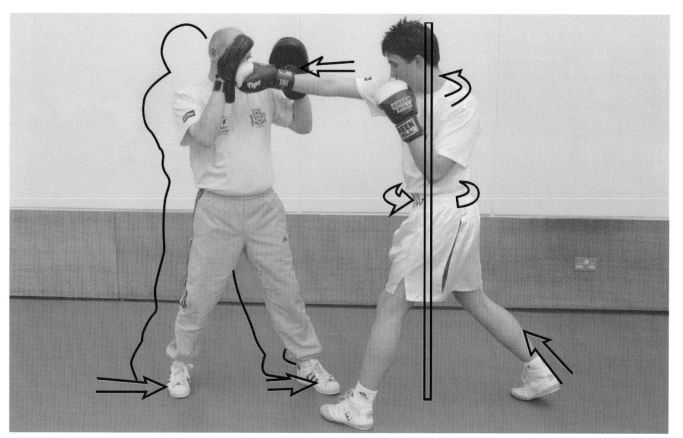

All boxers should be able to lead or counter to the body as well as to the head. Straight punches should be thrown in line with the shoulders and land above the belt. Power comes from an explosive drive from your feet and twisting of your trunk. The position of your front foot is important to ensure a solid contact with the target.

The left jab to body

Coaching hints

- Ensure that your shoulder is in line with the target before throwing the punch.
- Take special care to maintain a high guard, especially with your non-punching hand.
- Footwork must be fast, both in moving into and out of range.
- Practise moving in behind the jab, which is especially effective.

Sparring: try it as an attacking punch; as part of a 'switch attack' combination (body–head or head–body); or as a counter after triggering off an attack from your partner.

▲ *Left jab to the body*

The straight right to body

The straight right to the body is a powerful counter. It is also effective in switch attack combinations, but should rarely be used as a lead.

Switch of attack

Having practised straight punching to the body, you can switch the attack from head to body and body to head. The lead to the head could be a feint, with a jab to the body being the 'real' punch to follow. The two-punch combination could involve switching the attack of the second punch.

Straight right to the body ▶

The left hook

The left hook is usually used as a counter-punch – a punch thrown in reply to an opponent's lead following evasive action. As the name suggests, it is a bent-arm punch thrown by driving the body in an explosive twisting action. In the early stages learning to throw the left hook at an angle of 45 degrees to the floor should develop the right action.

The knuckle part of your glove must be in contact with the target as it lands. You can practise on a coaching pad held by a partner or coach. The left arm remains bent throughout the punch and the right side is kept firm.

Coaching hints

- Drive off the left foot.
- Let the body pull the arm through.
- Feel the arm relax until the last few inches.
- Keep the chin behind the shoulder, watching the punch as it lands.
- Protection comes from the high guarding right glove, with elbow tucked in.
- Once you have learnt the basic left hook, try throwing the punch to head and body.
- Southpaw boxers should follow the same coaching points for the right hook.

22

▲ *Left hook to the head* ▶
Note change of angle of pad and punch

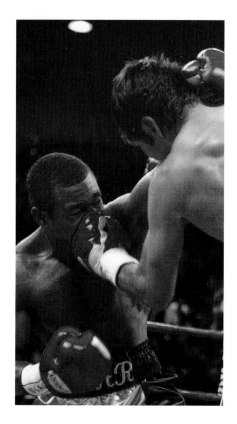

Uppercuts

Uppercuts with either hand are mechanically different to the straight and hook punches (that are thrown by pivoting around a central axis). The uppercut is thrown in an 'upward surge' from the floor, following the drive from the right or left leg. With the basic mid-range uppercut the arm follows a vertical path, while keeping a 90-degree bend.

Uppercuts are mainly counter punches, ideal against a committed or crouching opponent, or as part of close range combinations.

Practice

The vertical surface of traditional punch bags are not ideal for training; more recent wall bags with tailor-made indented surfaces make far more realistic targets. Partner work and coach pads provide the best practice, offering a variety of situations. Mirror work is essential:

- to check technique and the vertical path
- to check there is no obvious 'telegraph' or big wind-up to the punch, which will act as a signal to your opponent.

▲ *Right uppercut to the head*

▲ *Left uppercut to the head*

Defences

The art of boxing is to hit your opponent without being hit yourself. There are several defences which can be used against any one punch. A boxer should acquire as many defensive techniques as he can, selecting the ones he needs against a particular type of opponent. Similarly, most defences can be used against several punches. The 'push away' is a good example.

Each defence should be practised separately with the speed of attack slowed. Gradually, as your confidence increases, the punch can be thrown at a realistic speed. Timing your defensive action is as important as timing your attack. It could be that the 'attack' is really a feint. Generally, you should leave your defensive move as late as possible to ensure that your opponent is committed.

Coaching hints

- Where possible, take your target outside your opponent's line of attack – as in the side step.
- Balance must be kept at all times, so you are ready for a possible second or third punch.
- Keep defensive moves 'small': don't reach with the block; slip just outside the punch; push just out of range.

The numerous defence variations fit into 3 main areas:

1 **Blocks and parries**: using the hands, arms and shoulders to block or deflect punches.
2 **Use of footwork**: 'push away', 'side-steps' and 'pivots'.
3 **From the waist**, a positive defence (leaving both hands free to counter), eg 'duck', 'slip'.

Examples of defence follow. Once you have learned a defensive technique, try it against a variety of punches.

◀ *Outside parry to left jab*

Blocks and parries

▲ *Blocking your opponent's jab to the head*

▲ *Elbow block against a jab to the body*

The feet

▲ Use of the feet
Side step against a left jab to the head

▲ Use of the feet. The 'push away' against a left jab to the head.
Back foot moves first; front foot follows same distance

Evasive action at the waist

Note that the guard remains high and the balance is kept despite the upper body movement. Watch your opponent throughout the defensive moves to ensure that your head does not adopt a dangerous position.

◀ *Ducking under a left jab*

▲ *Slipping inside a left jab to the head*

▲ *Slipping outside a left jab to the head*

Infighting

The shorter the boxer, the more he will need to learn the art and craft of infighting – close-quarter boxing. Not only must he be able to move into the inside position and throw a variety of short-range punches, he must also learn how to move away with safety. His taller opponent will need to practise the skills involved as well. His aim is to stop his opponent from scoring and to move out of the close-quarter exchange as quickly as possible.

You should practise a variety of punches individually and then in combinations – clusters of punches. Straight punches, hooks and uppercuts may be thrown to both head and body. Being close to your opponent means that you cannot fully extend your arms. Then, greater emphasis should be placed on twisting the trunk to increase power.

The boxer who gets his arms inside his opponent's generally controls the scoring at close quarters. From this position he can score while effectively preventing the opponent from scoring. However, care must be taken with this and the position of the head to ensure that the rules are not being infringed.

Position of the feet: although they should adopt a more square-on position, some depth must be maintained to keep your balance.

▲ *Right uppercut to the head*

▲ *Right uppercut to the body*

▲ *Right hook to the head*

Covering

A sudden two-fisted attack can often force a boxer into a corner of the ring to regain his composure. There will be an immediate need for him to go on the defensive, before deciding on his counter-attack. Covering provides the defence needed.

There are three basic positions to adopt as a cover. Every boxer should try each one before deciding which suits his individual style and build. Practice with a partner throwing light punches will soon build up the confidence you need.

Once the immediate onslaught has passed, you should launch the counter-attack. It needs to be emphasised that covering is a defensive manoeuvre, to be carried out for as short a time as possible.

▲ *Full cover*

▲ *Half cover*

▲ *Cross cover*

▲ *While the defender is covering here, note it is entirely negative, with the eyes not on opponent and head in potentially illegal position*

Combination punching

Having mastered the basic punches individually, combining them in clusters follows. A combination may comprise two, three, four or more punches, and can include switch of attack. Timing, rhythm, speed and accuracy are essential.

Attention should always be given to sliding your feet into the correct position for the punch to follow, and ensuring that your non-punching hand is held in a high guarding position.

The best known combination is the 'one-two' to the head. A light, measuring jab is thrown at the target and a fast right follows, driven off the back foot with the right side pivoting through. The southpaw boxer would throw his right hand first with the left following. The same combination can be thrown to the body. Particular attention has to be paid to the guard and the back foot sliding forward, keeping the attacking boxer on balance.

▲ *The 'one-two' to the head thrown on coaching pads*
Note: • Contrasting commitment between the two punches
• The front foot finding range

▲ *Jab to body, jab to head*

▲ *(1) Jab to head – (2) left hook to body – (3) left hook to head – (4) right uppercut to head combination*
An advanced four-punch combination; (2) is as a counter combination after slipping inside the jab

(4)

Coaching hints

Shadow-boxing is a good way of working out combinations. Before sparring, it may help to decide on which combination to try; after sparring, it can be used to go over and improve the combinations used.

The feet must be in a position before each part of the combination lands, if the timing is to be accurate.

Relaxation is vital to help speed and rhythm. Power should be emphasised only in the final punch of a combination.

Beginning a combination with a jab has advantages, as has finishing the combination with the leading hand. Hence, the orthodox boxer might finish with a left hook and the southpaw with a right hook. This would 'close' the target, rather than leave him square-on and open to his opponent's attack. Variety of combinations is essential. A boxer should practise basic combinations, but also experiment with developing his own. A wide range of combinations will follow.

Countering

Countering is scoring when you have defended yourself successfully against your opponent's attack. Any defensive movement can be followed by a counter. Control of speed and power of punch are needed in the early practices to make sure that the counters are thrown correctly.

A start is best made by practising counters against the jab to the head. As soon as the correct 'feel' of the counter is acquired, you can increase speed. Straight punching should be tried first, then hooks, and lastly uppercuts.

The punch you choose to counter depends on which defence you used. Generally, the hand not used in the defensive action will be the one to counter with, or begin the counter-attack. Boxers should try to work out which is the best defence to use, and which counters could follow.

More advanced counters can be thrown either as single shots or combinations. The target can be switched from head to body, or body to head. Different types of opponent call for different counters, so you will need to try them out against a variety of sparring partners.

▼ *Jab counter after stepping outside your opponent's lead*

▲ *Right cross counter over your opponent's lead*

▼ *Straight right to the body counter, having ducked under your opponent's right*

▲ *Left hook to body counter after stepping inside left jab to the head*

▶ *(top) Push away against jab to the head; (bottom) Push back and counter with left jab to the head*

Southpaws

Southpaw boxers particularly need to develop the art of feinting the attack. Sideways movement is especially effective once an orthodox opponent's lead has been triggered off. The illustration on page 41 shows a southpaw moving to the right to throw a 'long-range' right hook from outside his opponent's line of attack.

Coaching hints

All the orthodox technique points apply.

• To the orthodox boxer a southpaw seems to be the 'wrong way round'. Take advantage of this – practise moves which will confuse and exasperate him.
• Switching attack is especially effective, as well as changing direction.
• When feinting, watch your opponent's reaction to a punch. Then decide on your counter – knowing how he will react to the feint.
• Most orthodox boxers throw straight rights or left hooks against southpaws; be ready for either and practise your defences.
• Try to make your opponent move the way you want him to in the ring; control and dictate the bout with your feet. Make him move onto your favourite punch!

▲ *The southpaw jab to the head*

▲ *The southpaw right hook to the head*

▲ *The southpaw straight left*

Training

Not only must a boxer be skilful, he also needs to be fit. He needs the stamina to keep going; the speed of punch and of defensive moves; the explosive drive from the feet. His body must be strong, his eye quick to see an opening. Running, circuit training and gym work will help him achieve this fitness. Each has a different part to play in a fitness programme; neglecting just one will leave a boxer unable to keep his skills flowing all the way through a spar or contest.

Running (*see* page 43): will range from 'steady state', fartlek and sustained runs, to high-quality interval runs and speed endurance runs. The final 'sharpening' will come from speed runs.

Gym work (*see* page 43): from aerobic to anaerobic workouts. The build-up should be gradual, and skill should always remain paramount.

Strength: starting with general strength and building to more specific.
- Fixed load circuits: individual and 'ton- up' – time taken should be recorded regularly to mark progress.
- Target circuits: the maximum repetitions in a set time. These will be specific, tailored exercises.
- Agility circuits.
- Weight training: power, strength and muscle endurance circuits.
- Groundwork: this is compensatory work, strengthening the neck, stomach, back, hands, etc., and is often isometric (held contractions).
- Plyometrics (explosive movements).
- Flexibility and PNF work.

All of the above training must be preceded by appropriate warm-up routines.

Skill acquisition

The approach will vary with the experience of the boxers. Amateur boxing is not just an open skill, it is *the* open skill, so teaching sound technique is only part of the coach's work. He then has to ensure the techniques are practised in many situations and against many possible styles of opponents.

Methods

- Technical sparring (practising one technique – the 'how').
- Conditioned sparring (the 'when' – situations varied).
- Open sparring (developing thinking and tactical awareness).
- Themed equipment work (themed to individual's strengths/weaknesses).
- Pad work (with coach/partner).
- Drills (individual and partner).
- Video analysis.

Running

Training for boxing is not only done in the gym or ring. All boxers should aim to run two to three times a week.

Start with gentle jogging for 10 minutes, gradually increasing to 20 minutes. You can use a test run of three to five kilometres (two or three miles) to check your progress. If you record your times, an occasional run over the same course will show how much you are improving. If there is no running track available, you can use trees – or even lamp posts on a street – as markers for 'speed bursts'.

Running over varying distances at different speeds will help build up general stamina and leg strength.

Gym work

Gym training is where the really hard work takes place – the hard work that makes the champion boxers. Each gym session should include both skill exercises and fitness training. Skills should be practised and repeated until they can be used smoothly and efficiently. Only with regular fitness training will a boxer achieve the all-round fitness he needs. Strength, speed and endurance are just some of the aspects of fitness required. Every boxer needs the physical capacity to box without tiring and the mental agility to 'read' his opponent. Then he can anticipate his next move and summon up the strength and speed of punch required. A boxer should prepare for each fight as if for the hardest possible contest, whatever the standard of his opponent.

Correct use of boxing equipment will improve fitness and promote boxing skills. Rounds should be timed with set periods of rest, however when working on skills, a beginner should rest/recover regularly, to avoid becoming tired and faulty patterns developing in his style as a result. It is best to practice only in good form – *never* sacrifice quality for quantity.

Each piece of equipment offers a different challenge. Your coach will help work out a training schedule to suit your particular needs, but in all gym work skill must be emphasised.

Shadow-boxing/mirror work

- Check the position of the guard and feet; the punch follows the feet.
- Watch for 'telegraphing' of moves. If you can see it, so will your opponent.
- Practise feinting before attacking; make feints realistic, and attack at speed.
- Go over the points made by your coach; try your own ideas by watching yourself first.

Maize ball

- Work mainly with straight punches, but hooks and uppercuts with either hand can be used.
- Move in all directions, especially circling left and right, always able to punch with either hand.
- Try two- and three-punch combinations, making sure that the feet slide in before each punch.
- Think of the problems experienced in a recent spar; work out some of the answers.

Bagwork

- Straight punches to the head and body should be thrown straight – in line with the shoulders, striking the bag as it comes.
- Single and combination punches should emphasise speed and power of attack.
- Vary the attack constantly, with an eye to doing the unexpected on occasion.
- Quality of punching is vital; feel the knuckle part of the closed glove landing solidly.
- Take care not to switch off when moving away.

Skipping

- Balance and footwork rhythm will be greatly aided; try skipping to music.
- Keep the body as relaxed as possible; never watch the feet.
- Try alternate leg and 'feet together' actions with single and double turns.
- Vary with pattern of leg movements, skip in all directions.

Wall bag

- Ideal for judgement of distance, changing angles of attack and moving away (varied footwork patterns), and varying the angle and range of punches.

44

Sparring and coaching

Sparring is the most important part of your training programme, putting all the skills you have practised to the test. A good boxer makes his spar a vital part of his programme. You should practise moves and tactics against a variety of sparring partners, as each opponent presents a different challenge. Head-guards can be worn to aid confidence (and also to prepare amateur boxers for wearing head-guards in contests), and heavy gloves may be used to reduce impact force. A gumshield is essential.

Sparring strategy

- Keep your sparring partner guessing; be selective when punching – reduce the power.
- Concentrate on doing the basics well; master straight punching first.
- Vary your moves, but keep the essentials – good balance and sound footwork.
- Try changing tactics each round.

▲ *Sparring. The advantage of having a coach is that he can see mistakes from outside the ring. Having pointed out the mistakes, he can give you invaluable coaching – especially using coaching pads – and can also help you learn new moves. And of course praise where praise is due – it's good to be reminded of your good points*

45

Competition

The ultimate test for many boxers is to box against an opponent in a competitive bout; to pit their wits and skills over three or four rounds against an opponent matched according to age, weight and experience. Belonging to an official ABA club enables competitors to box in inter-club tournaments. The ABAE organises national championships for seniors and juniors; it also organises novice championships. For schoolboys, championships are organised by the Schools Amateur Boxing Association (SABA). There are also the NACYP national championships – National Association of Clubs for Young People – for junior boxers.

The referee controls the bout and ensures that the rules are observed. Scoring is done by three to five judges, depending on whether the contest is on a 'club show' or a championship stage. (For scoring, *see* page 9.) Each boxer is allowed two seconds, one of whom advises him between rounds.

Anyone interested in joining an ABA club should contact the relevant national organisation or the Schools ABA (*see* page 47), which will put him in touch with the nearest affiliated club.

Competition hints

Against a tall opponent

- Always keep a target moving, using the feet and movement from the waist.
- Try to draw his lead by feinting, step inside and counter to the body and head.
- Use the ring to cut him off in corners; move sideways as well as in a straight line.

Against a shorter opponent

- Concentrate on keeping in the middle of the ring, away from the ropes.

- Keep him at long range with good use of the jab.
- Straight punching will allow you to use your height and reach.

Against a southpaw opponent

- Try to force him to lead, but keep moving.
- Circle away from his stronger hand – usually his left.
- Look for the right-hand counter to the body or head, and the left hook over his southpaw lead.

Against a counter puncher

- Try to make him lead off by feinting or drawing.
- Focus on having the last punch of an exchange – 'counter the counter'.
- Break his rhythm by changing tempo – don't let him settle. Try some sustained pressure to unsettle.

Contacts

For further information on the subjects discussed in the book, and details of your nearest club, contact one of the organisations below:

Amateur Boxing Association of England Ltd (ABAE)
Colin Brown, Hon. Secretary
National Sports Centre
Crystal Palace
London SE19 2BB
Tel: 020 8778 0251
Fax: 020 8778 9324
email: hq@abae.org.uk

Irish ABA
Sean Crowley, Hon. Secretary
National Boxing Stadium
South Circular Road
Dublin 2
Ireland
Tel: 00 3531 4533371
Fax: 00 3531 4540777
email: iaba@eircom.net

Welsh ABA
Jack Watkins, Hon. Secretary
8 Erw Wen
Rhiwbina
Cardiff CF4 6JW
Wales
Tel: 02920 623 566

Amateur Boxing Scotland
Donald Campbell, Administrator
Strathdonan
High Street
Elgin IV30 1AH
Scotland
Tel: 01343 544718
email: donald@absboxing.fsnet.co.uk

Schools ABA
Dudley Savill
11 Beaconsfield Road
Ealing
London W5 5JE
Tel: 020 8840 5519

Referees and Judges (England)
John Ball
6 Saddlers Way
Raunds
Northants, NN9 6RS
Tel: 01933 625821

Boxing Board of Control Ltd (Professional Boxing)
Simon Block, General Secretary
The Old Library
Trinity Street
Cardiff CF10 1BH
Wales
Tel: 02920 367000
Fax: 02920 367019
email: sblock@bbbofc.com
website: www.bbbofc.com

Index